South Africa

PHILIP GUPTE

AuthorHouse™
1663 Liberty Drive
Bloomington, IN 47403
www.authorhouse.com
Phone: 1 (800) 839-8640

Published by AuthorHouse 06/28/2018

ISBN: 978-1-5462-4883-5 (sc)
ISBN: 978-1-5462-4884-2 (e)

authorHOUSE®

"The World is a Book and Those Who do not Travel Read only One Page"
— Saint Augustine

About the Author

Philip Gupte used to work as a Professor of chemistry. Travel is his passion, he has travelled thru 98 countries and seen every major attraction in USA and many world wonders such as Taj Mahal, Pyramids, Statue of Christ in Brazil, Buckingham Palace, Windsor Castle, Tower Bridge, Westminster Abbey, Princess Diana's memorial (London), Eiffel Tower (France), Colosseum and Trevi Fountain (Rome, Italy), Vatican City (Rome), Brandenburg Gate, Berlin's Broken Wall (Berlin), Great Barrier Reef (Australia), Grand Canyon, Niagara Falls, Arch in St. Louis, Disneyland, Universal Studios, Bush Gardens, Colonial Williamsburg (Virginia), Lake Tahoe, Carlsbad Caves (New Mexico), San Jacinto Bay, Battleship Texas (Houston), Golden Gate Bridge, Alcatraz (San Francisco) and French Quarters (New Orleans).

Dedication

"To my Mother and Late Father"

Nelson Mandela Museum, Cape Town

"While Nelson Mandela is the father of South Africa, Mahatma Gandhi is our grandfather"

- Harris Majeke (South Africa's ambassador to India).

Prison cell where Nelson Mandela
lived for 25 years

Boat going towards Robben Island in Atlantic

Boat going towards Robben Island in Atlantic

Prison, Robben Island, in
Atlantic near Cape Town

Windhoek, capital of Namibia

Namibia was a German colony.

Windhoek, capital of Namibia

Namibia was a German colony.

Victoria falls, on the border of Zimbabwe and Zambia

Placid Zambezi river flows from Zambia into Zimbabwe.

Near Victoria Falls

This Falls was first discovered by British people. They named it Victoria Falls after the Queen of England Victoria who was the queen that time.

Near Victoria Falls

Victoria Falls is on the border of Zimbabwe and Zambia. Rhodesia was a British Colony, in 1964 Northern Rhodesia gained independence and now known as Zambia. In 1980, Southern Rhodesia became independent and now known as Zimbabwe.

Cape Town, South Africa

Crocodile park in Zimbabwe

Crocodile park in Zimbabwe

African Safari

Safari in Zimbabwe

Safari in Zimbabwe

Apartheid museum in
Johannesburg, South Africa

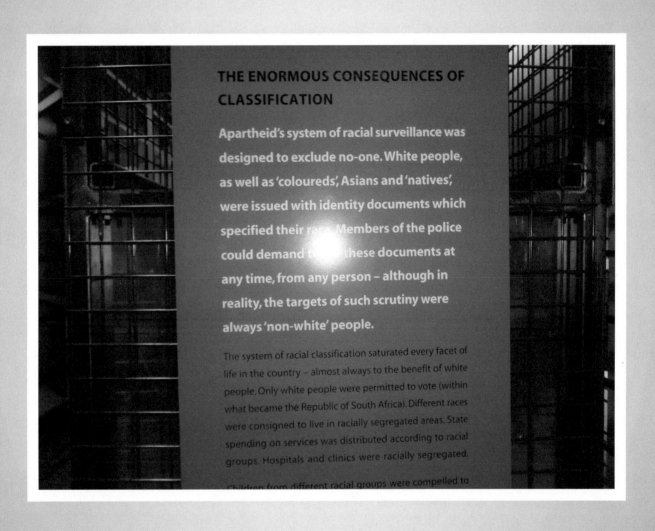

THE ENORMOUS CONSEQUENCES OF CLASSIFICATION

Apartheid's system of racial surveillance was designed to exclude no-one. White people, as well as 'coloureds', Asians and 'natives', were issued with identity documents which specified their race. Members of the police could demand to see these documents at any time, from any person – although in reality, the targets of such scrutiny were always 'non-white' people.

The system of racial classification saturated every facet of life in the country – almost always to the benefit of white people. Only white people were permitted to vote (within what became the Republic of South Africa). Different races were consigned to live in racially segregated areas. State spending on services was distributed according to racial groups. Hospitals and clinics were racially segregated.

Children from different racial groups were compelled to

Johannesburg, South Africa

I've always wanted to have a book of pictures about South Africa.

Gandhi lived in South Africa for about twenty-one years. He fought for equal rights of all non-white people. He later moved to India and fought for the independence of India, and because of him, the whole British Empire collapsed (lost all their colonies). He was called Mahatma Gandhi. Mahatma means "great soul" in Indian language.

Martin Luther King Jr. (USA) and Nelson Mandela (South Africa) both got inspiration from Gandhi, and they also fought for equal rights of non-white people. They both got Nobel Prize, but Gandhi never got one.

Printed in the United States
By Bookmasters